Killing The
Rising Sun:

How America Vanquished World War II
Japan

Study
Guide

Authored By

Slim Reads

FREE GIFT SPECIAL REPORT

The Tidiest and Messiest Places on Earth

After reading this summary you may conclude that the Middle East seems like a mess, but we made a special report about the Tidiest and Messiest Places on Earth! This report is a great supplement to that summary that is all about the virtues of being tidy.

As our **free gift** for being a **SLIM READS enthusiast** we are happy to give you a special report about the **3 Most Messy** and the **3 Most Tidy** places on Earth.

Learn about everything from **Garbage Island** to Computer-Chip **Clean Rooms** (and, of course, everything in between).

Get your **free copy** at:

http://sixfigureteen.com/messy

ISBN-10: 1537418688
ISBN-13: 978-1537418681

DISCLAIMERS

- Absolutely nothing in this volume is meant to constitute legal, financial, or medical advice nor are the opinions presented to be considered expert opinions.
- This volume is **NOT** meant to be a replacement for the original book, we believe our summation, key quotes and highlight analysis will increase interest in the complete book and not detract from it.
- In this volume, each particular detail is presented to the best of our knowledge and understanding of the recent book on WWII. If you think any of our analysis, or review is inaccurate **please email us** and we will correct it and publish an updated edition after we verify the inconsistency (slimreads@gmail.com).
- Most importantly: absolutely no portion of this summation volume was written in a Starbucks.

CONTENTS

WILL O'REILLY EVER RUN OUT OF THINGS TO KILL?

Will Bill O'Reilly ever run out of things to kill? After Jesus, Lincoln and Kennedy it looked like the well might run a little dry. Would there be a Killing Taft? With the release of Killing Reagan earlier this year, O'Reilly expanded the parameters of the series to include attempted assassinations. In this most recent incarnation, Killing The Rising Sun, about America's defeat of World War II Japan, the Killing series has become an umbrella historical banner, able to incorporate any historical figure, time period or event.

More than just a series of books, the sheer popularity of the Killing series has reshaped America's perceptions of our past. The way Band of Brothers and Saving Private Ryan shapes our view of America's invasion of Europe, or Downton Abbey effects how we view the early 20th century, or Mad Men shapes our view of New York City in the 1960s, Bill O'Reilly may be the most successful (and influential) murderer of our time.

This Study Guide will give you an insight into what you can expect from the upcoming Rising Sun release from O'Reilly. Even after its release this book will help to give some historical perspective that will continue to complement the reading of his latest volume.

WHY KILLING'S SO SUCCESSFUL

From the 1950s newsreel documentaries (like Victory at Sea) about the battles of World War II, to the creation of the History Channel in 1995, TV has always looked to the past. In recent years there has been a resurgence of historical programs – AMC'S Turn: Washington's Spies; HBO's Lyndon B. Johnson movie "All The Way"; History's Hatfields & McCoys, Texas Rising and the retelling of Roots; not to mention National Geographic Channel's movies based on Bill O'Reilly's bestselling Killing series of books, including Killing Kennedy, Killing Lincoln and Killing Jesus.

By 2012, O'Reilly had nine No. 1 books on contemporary issues [including The No Spin Zone and Culture Warrior]. When his publisher, HarperCollins, asked for a sequel to his auto-biography, A Bold Fresh Piece of Humanity, he instead suggested entering the history realm. He and his writing partner, Martin Dugard, came up with the Killing series. Harper turned it down and Henry Holt & Company ended up publishing it. It became one of the bestselling nonfiction book series in the world.

How successful has it been? Each of the "Killing" books has sold more than 1 million copies. O'Reilly's most popular installment in the series was "Killing Lincoln" – more than 2 million hardcover and audio versions were sold. (The Nielson BookScan figirues do not include downloads of e-books).

With Killing Kennedy, O'Reilly has not necessarily bought into the lone killer theory. Just read the end of the book when, s a reporter some years back, he went to interview Marina Oswald's Russian male friend! The man had been subpoenaed to testify when the JFK assassination case was brought up again for Congressional review. The guy killed himself… while

O'Reilly was at the door! And there is evidence the man had previously phoned the CIA asking for protection. Eh, that all seems pretty drastic for someone who was innocent of any involvement. JFK was killed by Oswald, but someone else was involved. Someone or some organization.

KILLING THE RISING SUN: Know Thy Enemy

Before we can fully appreciate America's losses and triumphs in the South Pacific during World War II, let's get a rough idea of the people, culture and philosophy American troops would be going up against. Many societal differences would set Japan's army apart from America's, making for a relentless and deadly foe. One philosophical hallmark of the Japanese army was that of BUSHIDO.

Bushido: Rectitude or Justice

Bushido not only refers to martial rectitude, but to personal rectitude: Rectitude or justice is the strongest virtue of Bushido. A well-known samurai defines it this way: "Rectitude is one's power to decide upon a course of conduct in accordance with reason, without wavering; to die when to die is right, to strike when to strike is right." Another speaks of it in the following terms: Rectitude is the bone that give firmness and stature. Without bones the head cannot rest on top of the spine, nor hands move nor feet stand. So, without Rectitude, neither talent nor learning can make the human frame into a samurai."

Courage

Bushido distinguishes between bravery and courage: Courage is worthy of being counted among virtues, only if it is exercised in the cause of Righteousness and Rectitude. In his Analects, Confucius says, "Perceiving what is right and not doing it reveals a lack of Courage." In short, "Courage is doing what is right."

Benevolence or Mercy

A man invested with the power to command and the power to kill was expected to demonstrate extraordinary powers of benevolence and mercy: Love, magnanimity, affection for others, sympathy and pity, are traits of Benevolence, the highest attribute of the human soul. Both Confucius and Mencius often said the highest requirement of a ruler of men is Benevolence.

Politeness

Discerning the difference between obsequiousness and politeness can be difficult for casual visitors to Japan, but for a true man, courtesy is rooted in benevolence: Courtesy and good manners have been noticed by every foreign tourist as distinctive Japanese traits. But Politeness should be the expression of a benevolent regard for the feelings of others; it's a poor virtue if it's motivated only by a fear of offending good taste. In its highest form, politeness approaches love.

Honesty and Sincerity

True samurai, according to author Nitobe, disdained money, believing that "men must grudge money, for riches hinder wisdom." Thus children of high-ranking samurai were raised to believe that talking about money showed poor taste, and that ignorance of the value of different coins showed good breeding: Bushido encouraged thrift, not for economic reasons so much as for the exercise of abstinence. Luxury was thought to be the greatest menace to manhood, and severe simplicity was required of the warrior class; the counting machine and abacus were abhorred.

Honor

Though Bushido deals with the profession of soldiering, it is equally concerned with non-martial behavior: The sense of Honor, a vivid consciousness of personal worth and dignity, characterized the samurai. He was born and bred to value the duties and privileges of his profession. Fear of disgrace hung like a sword over the head of every samurai. To take offense at slight provocation was ridiculed as 'short-tempered.' As the popular adage put it: "True patience means bearing the unbearable."

PELELIU – TROPICAL ISLAND BATTLEFIELD

Part 1 – The Point at Peleliu

Throughout the Marines landing and into the battle, the Japanese fortress located on top of "The Point" would continue to be the cause of large numbers of casualties on the beaches. COL Chesty Puller ordered Captain George Hunt (in command of Kilo Company, 3rd Bat, 1st Marines) to take the position. Captain Hunt would approach the objective short on supplies and under-gunned. One of his platoons would be pinned down for almost a full day in a location between fortifications. The Japanese would then cut a hole in his line leaving the company's right flank exposed.

Part 2 – Bloody Nose Ridge

Once "The Point" was captured and held by the 1st Marines, they would move on to take what became known as "Bloody Nose Ridge" or the Umurbrogol pocket. Colonel Puller led his marines in a number of attacks on the ridge, but they were repeatedly repulsed by the embedded Japanese forces, As the Marines slowly advanced through the narrow paths between the ridges, they took fairly high casualties. The Japanese snipers then started to target the American stretcher bearers. At night, the Japanese would infiltrate the American defensive lines to attack the Marines would use two-man foxholes to allow one person to sleep and the other to keep watch.

Part 3 – Hard Fighting at Peleliu

Over the full course of the battle, Colonel Puller's 1st Marines would lose 1,749 of 3,000 men (more than a 60% casualty rate). General Roy Geiger would subsequently send elements of the 81st infantry Division to relieve the Marine regiment. The 321st Regiment Combat Team would make its landing on the west coast of Peleliu at the northern end of Umurbrogol mountain on September 23rd. The 321st, 5th, and 7th Marines would then take turns attacking Umurbrogol and would all suffer similarly high casualty rates.

Part 4 – Casualties and Legacy of the Battle of Peleliu

The Allies reached the tip of the northern peninsula on September 27th. The remaining Japanese forces were encircled and defeated on October 13. The operation to remove the soldiers who remained in their fortified caves was costly in terms of casualties, time and resources. The remaining islands of Palau surrendered on September 2, 1945, when Japan formerly surrendered to the U.S., formally ending World War II. Some 35,000 Japanese troops were on Koror and Babeldaob at the time of the surrender.

IWO JIMA

Between June and August 1944, U.S. forces captured the Mariana Islands. These islands provided bases for Boeing B-29 bombers to attack Japanese Home Islands (mainland Japan). Iwo Jima served as an early warning station to radio reports of the bombers to Japan. It was also used by Japan to stage air attacks on the Mariana Islands to disrupt the U.S. bombings of Japan. Between November 1944 and January 1945, the Japanese destroyed 11 B-29s and damaged an additional 43. Furthermore, Iwo Jima was used by Japanese naval units when they were in dire need of a safe place.

To eliminate the above mentioned problems and to provide a staging area for Operation Downfall, the eventual invasion of Japanese Home Islands, the U.S. decided to start an operation for the capture of Iwo Jima. It was given the code name Operation Detachment. U.S. intelligence sources were confident that it would not take more than a week for Iwo Jima to fall, unaware that Japan was preparing a deep and complex defense of the island. Battle of Iwo Jima lasted for 36 days and saw some of the fiercest fighting of the Pacific War.

Japan knew the importance of defending Iwo Jima. Its loss would facilitate American air raids against Japanese Home Islands. However, the Imperial Japanese Navy had already lost almost all of its power and could not prevent the U.S. from landing. Depleting air strength also meant the remaining warplanes had to be hoarded to defend Japanese Home Islands. With no available means to defend Iwo Jima, Japan decided to rely on the established defensive equipment in the area and check U.S. by delaying tactics to gain time for defense of the mainland.

Lieutenant General Tadamichi Kuribayashi was assigned the task of defending Iwo Jima. Knowing he couldn't win the battle, he aimed at inflicting heavy casualties on American forces to force them to reconsider invasion of Mainland Japan. His strategy was radically different from Japan's usual strategy of beach defense to face the landings directly. He used Defense in Depth military strategy which seeks to delay rather than prevent the advance of the attacker, buying time and causing additional casualties. A complex and elaborate defense was prepared. Among other things, an extensive system of tunnels was built to connect the prepared positions so that positions which had been cleared could be re-occupied. Numerous snipers and camouflaged machine gun positions were also set up.

On 15 June 1944 the U.S. Navy and the U.S. Army Air Forces began naval bombardments and air raids against Iwo Jima which continued till 19 February 1945, the day U.S. Marines landed on the beach marking the start of the Battle of Iwo Jima. The pre-landing bombardment carried on for around eight months. Though bunkers and caves were destroyed, the bombing had limited success as the Japanese were heavily dug-in and fortified. Kuribayashi's superiors had ordered him to erect some beach defenses and these were the only Japanese defenses that were destroyed.

DOUGLAS MacARTHUR

Douglas MacArthur (1880-1964) was born on 26 January, 1880 at Little Rock, Arkansas, third son of Captain Arthur MacArthur, an army officer who rose to lieutenant general, and his wife Mary Pinkney. Douglas entered the United States Military Academy, West Point, New York, in 1899 and graduated first in his class in 1903. As a junior engineer officer, he served in the Philippines, accompanied his father on a tour of Asia and commanded a company of engineers in Kansas. In 1913 he joined the General Staff of the War Department, Washington, and in 1914 took a prominent part in the Veracruz expedition in Mexico. He was a major at the War Department in 1917 when America entered World War I.

In August that year MacArthur was promoted colonel of infantry and made chief of staff of the 42nd ('Rainbow') Division, with which he served on operations in France from February 1918. As a brigadier-general (August 1918), he led the 84th Brigade in several offensives, then assumed command of the 42nd Division shortly before the Armistice was declared. Twice wounded, he had been conspicuous in the front line, and had won the Distinguished Service Cross (twice), the Distinguished Service Medal, the Silver Star (seven times) and various foreign decorations.

MacArthur's request for more American troops and up-to-date military equipment to defend the whole of the Philippines, Washington was not at this stage abandoning the Rainbow-5 war plan that relegated the defense of the Philippines to a lower priority than the defeat of Germany. National pride was involved in the defense of the Philippines, and while acknowledging that it would become a secondary theatre in the event of war with both Japan and Germany, the United States was not prepared to abandon the Philippines to the Japanese without a fight. Another persuasive factor was the availability of the new B-17 Flying Fortress heavy bomber for te defence of the Philippines.

The US Army Air Corps argued that it gave the United States the capability to strike with devastating effect at distant Japanese airbases and naval invasion forces before hostile planes and ships could reach the Philippines. Of course, that was only theory; the bomber had not seen military action at this time. Having secured Washington's support, MacArthur then dispersed his troops widely and thinly across nine of the major Philippine islands.

In doing so, he breached one of the cardinal rules of military tactics. He thought that the Japanese would be unlikely to attack the Philippines before April 1942, and had no realistic plan to defend the islands if the Japanese attacked earlier. His poor military judgement would ensure the piecemeal loss of almost one third of his army when the Japanese attack came, and the loss of vital equipment and supplies that should have been concentrated on the heavily fortified island of Corregidor and the Bataan Peninsula on the western side of Manila Bay.

The harrowing assault against Japanese troops on Red Beach at 10 A.M. on Oct. 20, 1944 marked the beginning of the liberation of the Philippines and the triumphant return of Douglas MacArthur, punctuating the victorious U.S. march across the Pacific following the December 7, 1941 Japanese attack on Pearl Harbor. Former private first class Smith with the U.S. Army's 96th Division mostly remembers most a photograph taken of him and seven friends in Hawaii shortly before the Leyte landing. By the end of the assault, four of the eight had been killed and three, including Smith, were wounded. 'They were dropping a lot of mortar (shells) on us," said Smith, a former private first class with the U.S. Army's 96th Division. "I remember saying to myself, 'What the hell am I doing here?'" As the 73-year-old Californian traveled a half century back in thought, U.S. Marines staged a mock assault on the beach in one of the largest ceremonies commemorating the 50th anniversary of the Pacific War. With tens of thousands of people watching under a scorching sun, dozens of soldiers ran through the surf and belly flopped onto the beach, pretending to return the fire of Japanese troops. An American actor, wearing MacArthur's trademark khaki uniform and aviator sun glasses, waded ashore from a landing craft as the general did half a century earlier, with Philippine President Sergio Osmena at his side.

OPPRENHEIMER
10 FACTS ABOUT THE BOMB

1. The aftermath of nuclear explosions is just as deadly and far-reaching; radioactive fallout from the Chernobyl nuclear plant reached as far as Wales and Scotland.
2. Since 1951, the United States has gone on to produce 67,500 nuclear missiles.
3. The combined explosions of Hiroshima and Nagasaki killed an estimated 120,000 people, forcing the immediate surrender of Emperor Hirohito in World War 2.
4. The United States conducted over a thousand nuclear tests between 1945 and 1992, with a primary health consequence of increased radiation exposure leading to cancer. It's estimated some 6,000 people will die from thyroid cancer as a result.
5. Eight countries, including the United States, Russia, United Kingdom, France, China, India, Pakistan, and North Korea are declared nuclear states, with an additional three suspected countries that remain undeclared.
6. The U.S. and Russia each have thousands of nuclear warheads on high alert, a term used to describe the readiness of said missiles for launching. In this case, it would be mere minutes.
7. The most powerful nuclear weapon ever detonated was the Tsar Bomba, a Russian

bomb with a cumulative power of over 50 megatons of TNT.

8. The United States' largest nuclear bomb has the combined detonation power of 200 million pounds of high explosives.

9. On average, regular sized nuclear weapons that detonate over a city would burn away around 40 to 65 square miles in the blink of an eye.

10. A large-scale nuclear war would put 150 million tons of smoke into Earth's atmosphere, creating a nuclear winter chillier than the Ice Age.

INVENTING THE BOMB

Under Oppenheimer's guidance, the laboratories at Los Alamos were constructed. There, he brought the best minds in physics to work on the problem of creating an atomic bomb. In the end, he was managing more than 3,000 people, as well as tackling theoretical and mechanical problems that arose. He is often referred to as the "father" of the atomic bomb (in 1944, the Oppenheimers' second child, Katherine -- called Toni -- was born at Los Alamos.) The joint work of the scientists at Los Alamos resulted in the first nuclear explosion at Alamagordo on July 16, 1945, which Oppenheimer named "Trinity."

TESTING THE BOMB

At 5:29:45 A.M. on July 16, 1945, the Manhattan Project came to an explosive end as the first atom bomb is successfully tested in Alamogordo, New Mexico. Plans for the creation of a uranium bomb by the Allies were established as early as 1939, when Italian émigré physicist Enrico Fermi met with U.S. Navy department officials at Columbia University to discuss the use of fissionable materials for military purposes. That same year, Albert Einstein wrote to President Franklin Roosevelt supporting the theory that an uncontrolled nuclear chain reaction had great potential as a basis for a weapon of mass destruction. In February 1940, the federal government granted a total of $6,000 for research. But in early 1942, with the United States now at war with the Axis powers, and fear mounting that Germany was working on its own uranium bomb, the War Department took a more active interest, and limits on resources for the project were removed.

Brigadier-General Leslie R. Groves, himself an engineer, was now in complete charge of a project to assemble the greatest minds in science and discover how to harness the power of the atom as a means of bringing the war to a decisive end. The Manhattan Project (so-called because of where the research began) would wind its way through many locations during the early period of theoretical exploration, most importantly, the University of Chicago, where Enrico Fermi successfully set off the first fission chain reaction.

But the Project took final form in the desert of New Mexico, where, in 1943, Robert J. Oppenheimer began directing Project Y at a laboratory at Los Alamos, along with such minds as Hans Bethe, Edward Teller, and Fermi. Here theory and practice came together, as the problems of achieving critical mass – a nuclear explosion – and the construction of a deliverable bomb were worked out.

Finally, on the morning of July 16, in the New Mexico desert 120 miles south of Santa Fe, the first atomic bomb was detonated. The scientists and a few dignitaries had removed themselves 10,000 yards away to observe as the first mushroom cloud of searing light stretched 40,000 feet into the air and generated the destructive power of 15,000 to 20,000 tons of TNT. The tower on which the bomb sat when detonated was vaporized.

FDR DIES - TRUMAN BECOMES THE PRESIDENT

President Franklin Delano Roosevelt passed away after more than three momentous terms in office, leaving Vice President Harry S. Truman in charge of a country still fighting the Second World War and in possession of a weapon of unprecedented and terrifying power. On a clear spring day at his Warm Springs, Georgia retreat, Roosevelt sat in the living room with Lucy Mercer (with whom he had resumed an extramarital affair), two cousins and his dog Fala, while the artist Elizabeth Shoumatoff painted his portrait.

According to presidential biographer Doris Kearns Goodwin, it was about 1 P.M. that the president suddenly complained of a terrific pain in the back of his head, collapsing unconscious. One of the women summoned a doctor, who immediately recognized the symptoms of a massive cerebral hemorrhage and gave the president a shot of adrenaline into the heart in a vain attempt to revive him. Mercer and Shoumatoff quickly left the house, expecting FDR's family to arrive as soon as word got out.

Another doctor phoned first lady Eleanor Roosevelt in Washington D.C., informing her that FDR had fainted. She told the doctor she would travel to Georgia that evening after a scheduled speaking engagement. By 3:30 P.M., though, doctors in Warm Springs had pronounced the president dead.

During Roosevelt's last week, he made his last visit to Springwood in the last week of March 1945, about two weeks before his death. At his own wish, he was buried near the sundial in the Rose Garden on April 15, 1945. It is reported that Franklin's last words were, "I have a terrific headache."

Here are 5 little known facts about one of the most known and highly regarded presidents of the United States.

1. **TRISKAIDEKAPHOBIA** – Try saying that ten times fast. Apparently the great FDR was afraid of the number thirteen. Good thing the Nazis didn't know that.
2. **A FAMILY BUSINESS** – Roosevelt was related to 11 other United States presidents by either blood or marriage.
3. **FRIENDLY FIRE** – While on route to a secret meeting with Stalin and Churchill, Roosevelt's ship was accidentally fired upon by the USS William D. Porter. Luckily no one was hurt, however the entire USS Porter was arrested and demoted.
4. **WANDERING EYE SYNDROM** – Apparently, Eleanor wasn't enough for FDR. It's reported that he also had a mistress named Lucy Rutherford. To make matters worse, Ms. Rutherford was Eleanor's social secretary.
5. **TELEVISION POTUS** – Roosevelt was the first President to speak on National Television when, on April 30th, 1938, his speech at the New York World's Fair was broadcasted.

PRESIDENT TRUMAN – SHOULD HE USE THE BOMB

For Truman, the choice of whether or not to use the atomic bomb was the most difficult decision of his life. Truman stated that his decision to drop the bomb was purely military. A Normandy-type amphibious landing would have cost an estimated million casualties. Truman believed that the bombs saved Japanese lives as well. Prolonging the war was not an option for the President. Over 3,500 Japanese kamikaze raids had already wrought great destruction and loss of American lives.

The President rejected a demonstration of the atomic bomb to the Japanese leadership. He knew there was no guarantee the Japanese would surrender if the test succeeded, and he felt that a failed demonstration would be worse than none at all. Even the scientific community failed to foresee the awful effects of RADIATION SICKNESS. Truman saw little difference between atomic bombing Hiroshima and FIRE BOMBING Dresden or Tokyo.

A second factor in Truman's decision was the legacy of Roosevelt, who had defined the nation's goal in ending the war as the enemy's "unconditional surrender," a term coined to reassure the Soviet Union that the Western allies would fight to the end against Germany. It was also an expression of the American temperament; the United States was accustomed to winning wars and dictating the peace. On May 8, 1945, Germany surrendered unconditionally to great rejoicing in the Allied countries. The hostility of the American public toward Japan was even more intense and demanded an unambiguous total victory in the Pacific. Truman was acutely aware that the country – in its fourth year of total war – also wanted victory as quickly as possible.

A skilled politician who knew when to compromise, Truman respected decisiveness. Meeting with Anthony Eden, the British foreign secretary, in early May, he declared: "I am here to make decisions, and whether they prove right or wrong I am going to make them," an attitude that implied neither impulsiveness nor solitude.

After being presented with Stimson's report, he appointed a blue-ribbon "Interim Committee" to advise him on how to deal with the atomic bomb. Headed by Stimson and James Byrnes, whom Truman would soon name secretary of state, the Interim Committee was a group of respected statesmen and scientists closely linked to the war effort. After five meetings between May 9 and June 1, it recommended use of the bomb against Japan as soon as possible and rejected arguments for advanced warning. Clearly in line with Truman's inclinations, the recommendations of the Interim Committee amounted to a prepackaged decision.

HIROHITO

Japan's longest-reigning monarch, Emperor Hirohito, was born Michinomiya Hirohito on April 29, 1901, in the Aoyama Palace in Tokyo, Japan. He was the first son of Crown Prince Yoshihito (later Emperor Taisho) and Princess Sadako (later Empress Teimei). As a child, Hirohito was separated from his parents, as was custom, and given an imperial education at the Gakushuin School, also known as the Peers' School. He later attended a special institute which conditioned him to become emperor and was formally given the title of crown prince on November 2, 1916. Years later, in 1921, he became the first crown prince of Japan to travel abroad and study, voyaging to Europe.

In November 1921, shortly after his return to Japan, Hirohito was appointed acting ruler of Japan due to his father's failing health. On January 26, 1924, he married Princess Nagako (later Empress Nagako), a distant cousin of royal blood. The couple would eventually have seven children.

On December 25, 1926, following the death of his father, Hirohito succeeded him as emperor, taking the 124th Chrysanthemum Throne. He was given the title "Showa"

("Enlightened Peace"), and was formally known as Showa Tenno.

Since the creation of the imperial mythos, every emperor before Hirohito was worshipped as a God, with lip service if not with sincere devotion. It was one of those state mandated beliefs that are ubiquitous in nations that have never experienced democracy.

Hirohito, given his intensive indoctrination and ever-cautious advisers, was anxious to preserve the dynasty. That, and not averting a wider war, was his main objective. There is no doubt that Hirohito – the man – wanted peace.

Hirohito's speech was delivered to the Japanese public. It was written specifically so that they could understand why Japan was surrendering. The only aspect of war they experienced and understood was aerial bombing. In Hirohito's rescript to Japanese soldiers and sailors, there was no mention of the nuclear bombs. It mentioned the Soviet declaration of war on Japan as the reason why Japan was terminating the war.

A postwar constitution preserved the monarchy, but defined the emperor as a mere symbol of the state. All political power went to elected representatives. Unlike many among his top military brass, Hirohito was not indicted as a war criminal, in part because U.S. authorities feared it could throw their occupation into chaos. From 1945 to 1951, Hirohito toured the country and oversaw reconstruction efforts. The American occupation ended in 1952, after which Hirohito served largely in the background.

After the war, the new constitution, drafted by the United States, transformed Japan into a constitutional monarchy, so that sovereignty lay with the people, instead of the emperor. Japan went through a period of rapid economic growth.

AFTERMATH: NORTH KOREA

After the division of Korea, Japan and the Republic of Korea (ROK) had established diplomatic relations. In December 1965, under the Treaty on Basic Relations between Japan and the Republic of Korea, Japan recognized South Korea as the only legitimate government of the whole Korean peninsula; Japan and South Korea are close neighbors. The Ministry of Foreign Affair of Japan explains their relationship as 'sharing fundamental values, such as freedom, democracy, respect for basic human rights, and common interests in maintaining regional peace and security'.

Due to various disputes, that relationship has greatly deteriorated in recent years; those disputes include the territorial claims on Liancourt Rocks (Dokdo or Takeshima), the Japanese prime ministers' visits to the Yasukuni Shrine, and different views on Imperial Japan's treatment of colonial Korea, as well as Japan's refusal to apologize or pay reparations for mistreatment of World War II comfort women from Korea. These tensions have complicated American efforts to promote a common front against Chinese threats in the region.

According to a 2014 BBC World Service Poll, 13% of Japanese view South Korea's influence positively, with 37% expressing a negative view, while 15% of South Koreans view Japanese influence positively, with 79% viewing it negatively, making South Korea the country with the second most negative perception of Japan in the world (after China).

While Japan's emperor was forced to admit publicly that he was, in fact, NOT a god the same was never demanded from the head of Korea. Korea was to Japan what Austria was to Germany. The Japanese viewed them as closer kin than the rest of Asia. Korea would be subordinate to Japan, for sure, but the leader of Korea was also viewed as a (albeit lesser) deity within Japan and Korea.

While South Korea democratized, North Korea continues to be ruled by the descendants of the supposed god-men that partnered with the Japanese Emperor during WWII. This is why when Kim Jung Ill died North Koreans went into morning. Even exiled North Koreans that had escaped the horrors of living there have been seen sobbing in the streets of China, Mongolia and South Korea when they heard the news.

FURTHER READING

Are you ready to quickly absorb the main points and highlights of the next best seller? Check out great summaries from these great brands,

Slim Reader and Slim Reads:

▰ If you liked this news guide you will LOVE our summary the latest Legends & Lies release. **LEGENDS & LIES: The Patriots**, pulls back the curtains and reveals what about the founders was fact and what was fiction; check out our summary here:
http://amzn.com/B01HORJIZE

▰ Looking for inspiration? Check out *Summary: Originals: How Non-Conformists Move the World | Summary & Highlights with BONUS Action Plan* is a great read, but it is a LONG book. We have already read it and summarized it for you so pick up a copy and enjoy:
http://amzn.com/B01DMVEQ12

▰ Got a taste for **Geo-Politics?** What's really going on in the Middle East? Check out *Summary: And Then All Hell Broke Loose*. Get the summary today:
http://amzn.com/B01C7HE4VE

FREE GIFT SPECIAL REPORT

10 Little-Known Facts Even Potterheads Don't Know

Pop quiz hot shot! You think you know EVERYTHING about the Harry Potter series and its amazing rise in worldwide fandom? THINK AGAIN! I'm sure you know your Dumbledores from your Longbottoms but it is time to push your fandom to the next level (that's right, level 9 and 3/4)!

As our **free gift** for being a **SLIM READS enthusiast** we are happy to give you a special report about the **10 Little-Known Facts Even Potterheads Don't Know**.

Don't let Voldemort keep you from getting this awesome report!

Get your **free copy** at:

http://sixfigureteen.com/potter

ALSO: We will let you know about future Slim Reads titles so this is **win-win**! Enjoy your **FREE GIFT** and thank you for being part of the **SLIM READS** Family!

FREE GIFT SPECIAL REPORT

The 10 Strange Deaths of Vladimir Putin

This election year, a major part of **Trump's foreign policy** message is that he will be able to work together with the Russian head-of-state Vladimir Putin, but what kind of man is Mr. Putin?

As our **free gift** for being a **SLIM READS enthusiast** we are happy to give you a special report about some of the mysterious and <u>strange deaths</u> that have befallen Mr. Putin's enemies.

Plane crashes, multiple stab wounds and radioactive sushi are just a few of the misfortunes that have befallen those who opposed the Russian President.

Get your free copy at:

http://sixfigureteen.com/putin

<u>ALSO</u>: We will let you know about future Slim Reads titles so this is win-win! Enjoy your FREE GIFT and thank you for being part of the SLIM READS Family!

FREE GIFT SPECIAL REPORT

The Tidiest and Messiest Places on Earth

We made a special report about the Tidiest and Messiest Places on Earth! This report is a great supplement to that summary that is all about the virtues of being tidy.

As our **free gift** for being a **SLIM READS enthusiast** we are happy to give you a special report about the **3 Most Messy** and the **3 Most Tidy** places on Earth.

Learn about everything from **Garbage Island** to Computer-Chip **Clean Rooms** (and, of course, everything in between).

Get your **free copy** at:

http://sixfigureteen.com/messy

ALSO: We will let you know about future Slim Reads titles so this is **win-win**! Enjoy your **FREE GIFT** and thank you for being part of the **SLIM READS** Family!

Made in the USA
San Bernardino, CA
29 November 2016